Office of Government Commerce

Key Element Guide
Service Transition

D1173008

London: TSO

information & publishing solutions

Published by TSO (The Stationery Office)
and available from:

Online
www.tsoshop.co.uk

Mail, Telephone, Fax & E-mail
TSO
PO Box 29, Norwich NR3 1GN
Telephone orders/General enquiries:
0870 600 5522
Fax orders: 0870 600 5533
E-mail: customer.services@tso.co.uk
Textphone: 0870 240 3701

TSO Shops
16 Arthur Street, Belfast BT1 4GD
028 9023 8451 Fax 028 9023 5401
71 Lothian Road, Edinburgh EH3 9AZ
0870 606 5566 Fax 0870 606 5588

TSO@Blackwell and other Accredited Agents

Published with the permission of the Office of
Government Commerce on behalf of the Controller
of Her Majesty's Stationery Office

First published 2008

ISBN 9780113310722 (Sold in a pack of 10 copies)
ISBN 9780113311217 (Single copy ISBN)

Printed in the United Kingdom for The Stationery
Office
N5745154   03/08

Contents

Acknowledgements

ITIL AUTHORING TEAM

- Sharon Taylor (Aspect Group Inc.) Chief Architect
- Shirley Lacy (ConnectSphere) Author
- Ivor Macfarlane (IBM) Author
- Jane Clark (ConnectSphere) Contributor

REVIEWERS

OGC would like to recognize the contribution of the following individuals:

Graham Barnett, Deirdre Conniss, Robert Falkowitz, Matiss Horodishtiano, Chris Jones, Siegfried Schmitt, Dean Taylor, Cheryl Tovizi and Paul Wigzel

and from *it*SMF's International Publications Executive Sub-Committee (IPESC):

Peter Brooks (Lead Assessor), Jorge Aballay (Argentina), Marianna Billington (NZ), Bart van Brabant (Belgium), Jenny Ellwood-Wade (NZ), Ashley Hanna (UK), David Salisschiker (Argentina), Robert Stroud (US) and Wilfred Wah (Hong Kong).

1 Introduction

This publication is intended to provide a synopsis of the basic concepts and practice elements of Service Transition, which forms part of the core ITIL Service Management Practices. These practices form the ITIL Service Lifecycle on which the concepts of these and all other ITIL Service Management publications are based.

This publication is not intended to replace the ITIL core publications and should not be used in place of the full practice guidance publications. The content in this publication is depicted at a high level and will not be practical as a substitute for the full guidance publication; rather it should serve as a handy quick reference that is portable and helps direct the reader to the full guidance information when needed.

1.1 THE ITIL FRAMEWORK

ITIL Service Management has been practised successfully around the world for more than 20 years. Over this time, the framework has evolved from a specialized set of service management topics with a focus on function to a process-based framework and now to a broader, holistic service lifecycle. The evolution and transformation of ITIL Service Management Practices is the result of the evolution of the IT service management (ITSM) industry itself, through knowledge, experience, technical innovation and thought leadership. The ITIL Service Lifecycle is both a reflection of the industry practice in use today, and concepts that will move us forward in the future of service management philosophies and practices.

The objective of the ITIL Service Management Practices framework is to provide services to business customers that are fit for purpose, stable and which are so reliable that the business views them as a trusted utility.

ITIL Service Management Practices offer best-practice guidance applicable to all types of organizations that provide services to a business. Each publication addresses capabilities having direct impact on a service provider's performance. The structure of the core practice takes form in a service lifecycle. It is iterative and multidimensional. It ensures organizations are set up to leverage capabilities in one area for learning and improvements in others. The core is expected to provide structure, stability and strength to service management capabilities with durable principles, methods and tools. This serves to protect investments and provide the necessary basis for measurement, learning and improvement.

The guidance in the ITIL framework can be adapted for use in various business environments and organizational strategies. The complementary guidance provides flexibility to implement the core in a diverse range of environments. Practitioners can select complementary guidance as needed to provide traction for the core in a given business context, in much the same way as tyres are selected based on the type of automobile, purpose and road conditions. This is to increase the durability and portability of knowledge assets and to protect investments in service management capabilities.

1.2 THE ITIL CORE PRACTICE PUBLICATIONS

The ITIL Service Management Practices comprise three main sets of products and services:

- Core guidance
- Complementary guidance
- Web support services.

1.2.1   ITIL Service Management Practices – core guidance

The core set consists of six publications:

- *The Official Introduction to the ITIL Service Lifecycle*
- *Service Strategy*
- *Service Design*
- *Service Transition*
- *Service Operation*
- *Continual Service Improvement.*

A common structure across all the core guidance publications helps the reader to find references between volumes and to know where to look for similar guidance topics within each stage of the lifecycle.

1.2.2   ITIL Service Management Practices – complementary guidance

This is a living library of publications with guidance specific to industry sectors, organization types, operating models and technology architectures. Each publication supports and enhances the guidance in the ITIL Service Management core. Publications in this category will be continually added to the complementary guidance library and will contain contributions from the expert and user ITSM community. In this way, ITIL Service Management Practices are illustrated in real-life situations and in a variety of contexts that add value and knowledge to your own ITIL practice.

1.2.3   ITIL Service Management Practices – web support services

These products are online, interactive services, which will develop over time and include elements such as the glossary of terms and definitions, the interactive service model, online subscriber services, case studies, templates and ITIL Live® – an interactive expert knowledge centre where users can access time with ITSM experts to discuss questions and issues, and seek advice.

Readers of this key element guide are encouraged to explore the entire portfolio of ITIL Service Management publications and services.

1.3   WHAT IS A SERVICE?

Service management is more than just a set of capabilities. It is also a professional practice supported by an extensive body of knowledge, experience and skills. A global community of individuals and organizations in the public and private sectors fosters its growth and maturity. Formal schemes exist for the education, training and certification of practising organizations, and individuals influence its quality. Industry best practices, academic research and formal standards contribute to its intellectual capital and draw from it.

> **Definition of a service**
> A service is a means of delivering value to customers by facilitating outcomes customers want to achieve without the ownership of specific costs and risks.

1.4   WHAT IS A LIFECYCLE?

The service lifecycle contains five elements, each of which relies on service principles, processes, roles and performance measures. The ITIL Service Lifecycle uses a hub and spoke design, with Service Strategy at the hub, and Service Design, Transition and Operation as the revolving lifecycle stages, anchored by Continual Service Improvement (Figure 1.1). Each part of the lifecycle exerts influence on the others and relies on the others for inputs and feedback. In this way, a constant set of checks and balances throughout the service lifecycle ensures that as business demand changes with business need, the services can adapt and respond effectively to them.

Figure 1.1 The ITIL Service Lifecycle

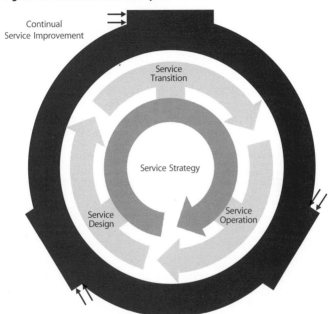

At the heart of the service lifecycle is the key principle – all services must provide measurable value to business objectives and outcomes. ITIL Service Management focuses on business value as its prime objective. Each practice revolves around ensuring that everything a service provider does to manage IT services for the business customer can be measured and quantified in terms of business value. This has become extremely important of late as IT organizations are required to operate as businesses in order to demonstrate a clear return on investment, equating service performance with business value to the customer.

2 The ITIL Service Management Model

The ITIL Service Lifecycle uses models to refine and customize an organization's use of the ITIL Service Management Practices. These models are intended to be reusable in a variety of organizational contexts and to help take advantage of economies of scale and efficiencies.

Central to these models are the overarching process elements that interact throughout the lifecycle and bring power and wisdom to service practices. These service model process elements consist of two main types – lifecycle governance and lifecycle operations. These are depicted in Figure 2.1.

Figure 2.1 Process elements of the ITIL Service Lifecycle

Service Lifecycle Governance Processes		Service Lifecycle Operational Processes		
Continual Service Improvement Processes	**Service Strategy Processes**	**Service Design Processes**	**Service Transition Processes**	**Service Operation Processes**
	Demand Management			
	Strategy Generation			
	Service Portfolio Management			
	IT Financial Management			
Service Measurement		Service Catalogue Management		
		Service Level Management		
		Capacity Management		
		Availability Management		
		Service Continuity Management		
		Information Security Management		
		Supplier Management		
Service Reporting			Transition Planning and Support	
			Change Management	
			Service Asset and Configuration Management	
			Release and Deployment Management	
			Service Validation and Testing	
			Evaluation	
			Knowledge Management	
Service Improvement				Event Management
				Incident Management
				Request Fulfilment
				Problem Management
				Access Management
				Operation Management

While these processes are non-linear, they do have a logical and sometimes sequential flow. To illustrate this, Figure 2.2 shows the high-level, basic flow of lifecycle process elements in the ITIL Service Lifecycle.

Figure 2.2 A high-level view of the ITIL Service Management Model

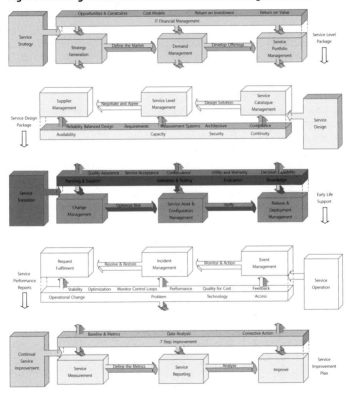

This publication deals with the high-level concepts drawn from the Service Transition stage of the service lifecycle.

3 Principles of Service Transition

3.1 PURPOSE, GOALS AND OBJECTIVES

3.1.1 Purpose

The purpose of Service Transition is to:

- Plan and manage the capacity and resources required to package, build, test and deploy a release into production and establish the service specified in the customer and stakeholder requirements
- Provide a consistent and rigorous framework for evaluating the service capability and risk profile before a new or changed service is released or deployed
- Establish and maintain the integrity of all identified service assets and configurations as they evolve through the Service Transition stage
- Provide good-quality knowledge and information so that Change, Release and Deployment Management can expedite effective decisions about promoting a release through the test environments and into production
- Provide efficient repeatable build and installation mechanisms that can be used to deploy releases to the test and production environments and be rebuilt if required to restore service
- Ensure that the service can be managed, operated and supported in accordance with the requirements and constraints specified within the Service Design.

3.1.2 Goals

The goals of Service Transition are to:

- Set customer expectations on how the performance and use of the new or changed service can enable business change

- Enable the business change project or customer to integrate a release into its business processes and services
- Reduce variations in the predicted and actual performance of the transitioned services
- Reduce the Known Errors and Problems and minimize the risks from transitioning the new or changed services into production
- Ensure that the service can be used in accordance with the requirements and constraints specified within the service requirements.

3.1.3 Objectives

The objectives of Service Transition are to:

- Plan and manage the resources to establish successfully a new or changed service into production within the predicted cost, quality and time estimates
- Ensure there is minimal unpredicted impact on the production services, operations and support organization
- Increase the customer, user and Service Management staff satisfaction with the Service Transition practices, including deployment of the new or changed service, communications, release documentation, training and knowledge transfer
- Increase proper use of the services and underlying applications and technology solutions
- Provide clear and comprehensive plans that enable the customer and business change projects to align their activities with the Service Transition plans.

3.2 PRACTICE

Service Transition builds, tests and deploys a release and establishes that the new or changed service will deliver the requirements specified by the customer and stakeholders.

Services are the means by which a business unit delivers value to one or more other business units, or to sub-units within itself, as shown in Figure 3.1. Business units that deliver services are referred to as service providers or service units.

Figure 3.1 Services provide value by increasing the performance of customer assets and removing risks

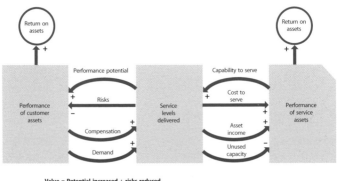

Value = Potential increased + risks reduced
Value ≥ Compensation

ROA = Compensation/Cost to serve

3.2.1 Service utilities and warranties

When transitioning a service it is important to understand how to test and evaluate the value that will be delivered to the customers and their business operations. From the customer's perspective, value can be deconstructed into two primary elements: service utility (what the service does) and the service warranty (how well it does it).

Service utility

Service utility is the commitment by the service provider that the functionality of the service will meet the agreed functional business requirements, i.e. it is fit for purpose. Utility is from the attributes of the service that have a positive effect on the performance of activities, objects and tasks associated with desired outcomes. Removal or relaxation of constraints on service performance is perceived as a positive effect.

Service warranty

Service warranty is the assurance that the service will deliver the expected business benefit to the customer. Warranty comes from the positive effect being available when needed, in sufficient capacity or magnitude, and dependably in terms of continuity and security.

> **Realizing expected value**
> Customers can only realize the expected value from something that is fit for purpose and fit for use.

3.2.2 Policies

The key policies of Service Transition are:

- Creating a formal policy for Service Transition
- Implementing all changes through Service Transition
- Adopting a common framework and standards
- Maximizing re-use of established processes and systems
- Aligning Service Transition plans with business needs
- Establishing and maintaining relationships with stakeholders
- Establishing effective controls and disciplines
- Providing systems for knowledge transfer and decision support
- Planning release and deployment packages
- Anticipating and managing course corrections
- Proactively managing resources across Service Transition
- Ensuring early involvement in the service lifecycle
- Assuring the quality of the new or changed services
- Proactively improving quality during Service Transition.

Release policy

A release policy is defined for transitioning one or more services. It includes:

- The unique identification, numbering and naming conventions for different types of release together with a description
- The roles and responsibilities at each stage in the release and deployment process
- The expected frequency for each type of release
- The approach for accepting and grouping changes into a release, e.g. how enhancements are prioritized
- The mechanism to automate the build, installation and release distribution processes to improve re-use, repeatability and efficiency
- Details of how the configuration baseline for the release is captured and verified against the actual release contents
- Exit and entry criteria and authority for acceptance of the release into each Service Transition stage and into the controlled test, training, disaster recovery and production environments
- Criteria and authorization to exit Early Life Support (ELS) and handover to Service Operation.

Service Validation and Testing policies

Policies that drive and support Service Validation and Testing include service quality policy, risk policy, Service Transition policy, release policy and Change Management policy.

3.3 KEY ELEMENTS

The scope of Service Transition includes the management and coordination of the resources to package, build, test and deploy a release into production and establish the service specified in the customer and stakeholder requirements.

The scope of the Service Transition lifecycle stage is shown in Figure 3.2. Service Transition activities are shown in the white boxes. The dark boxes represent activities in the other ITIL core lifecycle publications.

There may be situations when some activities do not apply to a particular transition. For example, the transfer of a set of services from one organization to another may not involve release planning, build, test and acceptance.

Figure 3.2 The scope of Service Transition

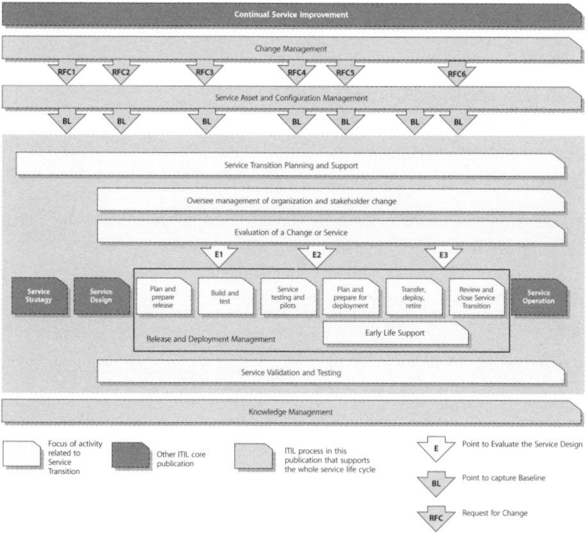

Service Transition uses all the processes described in the other stages of the service lifecycle as it is responsible for testing these processes, either as part of a new or changed service or as part of testing changes to the service management processes.

3.3.1 Processes that support the service lifecycle

The service lifecycle processes that are critical during the transition stage, but which support all lifecycle stages, are:

- Change Management
- Service Asset and Configuration Management (SACM)
- Knowledge Management.

3.3.2 Processes within Service Transition

The following processes are strongly focused within the Service Transition stage:

- Transition Planning and Support
- Release and Deployment Management
- Service Testing and Validation
- Evaluation.

Figure 3.3 illustrates the service provider assets used to deliver services to the business and customers.

Figure 3.3 Service assets used to deliver services

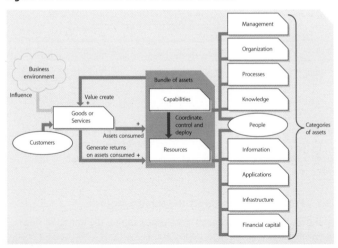

3.3.3 Service Transition inputs from Service Strategy

Inputs from Service Strategy influence the overall approach, structures and constraints that apply to Service Transition. They include:

- Service Portfolio, Customer Portfolio, Contract Portfolio
- Service model
- Policies, strategies
- Constraints
- Architectures
- Service Transition requirements
- Service Management plan (as required by ISO/IEC 20000).

3.3.4 Service Transition inputs from Service Design

Service Design develops the five aspects of Service Design in collaboration with customers, external and internal suppliers and other relevant stakeholders. These are:

- Services
- Service Portfolio
- Technology architectures and management systems
- Processes
- Measurement methods and metrics.

The Service Design is documented in a Service Design Package (SDP) that forms the key input to Service Transition. The SDP includes:

- Requirements (business requirements, service applicability, service contacts)
- Service Design
- Organizational Readiness Assessment report and plan
- Service Lifecycle plans
- Service Programme plan, covering all stages of the lifecycle of the service, including the timescales for the transition, operation and subsequent improvement of the service

- Service Transition plans, including overall transition strategy, objectives, policy, risk assessment and plans
- Service Operational Acceptance plan, covering the overall operational strategy, objectives, policy, risk assessment and plans
- Service Acceptance Criteria (SAC).

3.3.5 Service Transition outputs

Key outputs from Service Transition are to Service Operation, Continual Service Improvement and the customer and user community to whom services are delivered following successful Service Transition. These outputs include:

- Approved service release package and associated deployment packages
- Updated service package or service bundle that defines the end-to-end service(s) offered to customers
- Updated Service Portfolio and Service Catalogue
- Updated Contract Portfolio
- Documentation for a transferred or decommissioned service
- Suggestions and observations to improve processes for CSI
- Approved updated or new service.

3.3.6 Service Transition common operation activities

Managing organizational and stakeholder change

Cultural and organizational assessment and change design are the responsibility of Service Strategy and Service Design. However, most significant Service Transitions will have an effect on working practices and so require a change in the behaviour and attitudes of many teams and stakeholder groups.

Organizational adoption happens at two levels: individual and organizational. It is important to understand the culture of the organizations and the people involved. This can be quite diverse across different cultures and business units. Factors that drive successful change at the organization level include:

■ Leadership for the change
■ Organizational adoption
■ Governance process
■ Organization capabilities
■ Business and service performance measures
■ A strong communication process with feedback.

The Service Transition process owner or manager is a key stakeholder and needs to be proactive in reporting issues and risks to the change leaders, e.g. when the volume of changes may impact Service Operation's ability to keep the services running.

If issues arise, the process owner must reinforce the importance of consistency in the implementation of the changes. For example, communication should focus on messages that help people to:

■ Understand the need for knowledge and effective knowledge transfer
■ Understand the importance of making decisions at the right speed/ within the appropriate time
■ Understand the need to complete tests and perform reviews in a timely manner
■ Apply more effective risk assessment and management methods for Service Transition
■ Follow the deadlines for submitting changes and releases.

Any significant change delivers organizational change, occurring in incremental phases or rapidly affecting some or all of an organization, its people and its culture. Effective leaders and managers recognize this and plan accordingly.

It is important to understand the 'emotional stages' that a person needs to get through before acceptance. This is illustrated in Figure 3.4.

Figure 3.4 The emotional cycle of change

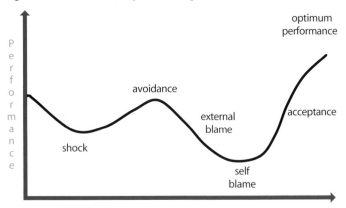

Managing communications and commitment

Communications need to be targeted at the right audience and clearly communicate the messages and benefits consistently. A range of communication options should be considered and used together for optimal effect.

The Service Transition team's goal is to build enthusiasm and commitment around the change. This rests on a full understanding of the impact of their work on others, and therefore tailoring the approach to the stakeholder audience.

3.4 ROLES AND RESPONSIBILITIES

A release that consists of many different types of service assets may involve many people, often from different organizations. The typical criteria for handover and acceptance of a release should be defined and then modified as required for specific transitions. The main roles and responsibilities at points of handover should be defined to ensure that everyone understands their role and level of authority as well as those of others involved in the release and deployment process.

Service Transition must be actively involved in changing the mindsets of people across the lifecycle to ensure they are ready to play their role in Service Transition. Key stakeholders include:

- Service Transition staff
- Customers
- Users
- Service Operation staff
- Suppliers.

The specific roles and responsibilities that relate primarily to Service Transition are:

- Service Transition management
- Planning and support
- Change Management
- SACM
- Performance and risk evaluation
- Service Knowledge Management
- Service test management
- Release and deployment
- Release packaging and build
- Deployment
- ELS
- Build and test environment management.

These roles will be used to some extent by other processes within the Service Management lifecycle. Depending on the size of the organization and the scope of the service being transitioned, some of these roles will be combined and performed by one individual. However, service test management and physical testing must always be performed by resources independent of other functions or processes.

3.5 SERVICE TRANSITION MODELS

3.5.1 Service model

A service model describes the structure and dynamics of how the new or changed service is operated and managed.

3.5.2 Integrated Service Transition model

A service may be deployed into the production environment in a number of ways. Service Design will select the most suitable service transition models that include the approach, mechanisms, processes, procedures and resources required to transition a service or change on time and within budget. These models provide repeatable ways of dealing with particular types of change, release and/or deployment. They help people to understand and learn from experience by sharing and re-using standard approaches. This improves planning and the ability to compare actual performance against predicted performance.

3.5.3 Process model

The generic process elements for a process model are described in the *Service Design* publication.

A process flow is a way of predefining the steps that should be taken to handle a process in an agreed way. Support tools can be used to manage the required process. An example of a process flow for a normal change that forms part of the change process model is shown in Figure 3.5.

Normal change model

Figure 3.5 Example of process flow for a normal change

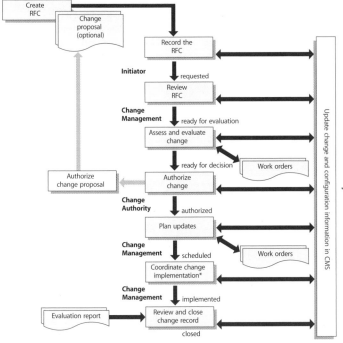

*Includes build and test the change

3.5.4 Change authorization model

Formal authorization is obtained for each change from a change authority, which may be a role, a person or a group of people. The levels of authorization for a particular type of change should be judged by the type, size or risk of the change, e.g. changes in a large enterprise that affect several distributed sites may need to be authorized by a higher-level change authority, such as a global Change Advisory Board (CAB) or the board of directors. Figure 3.6 provides an example of a change authorization model. Escalation procedures are also defined, e.g. who should be contacted and when.

Figure 3.6 Example of a change authorization model

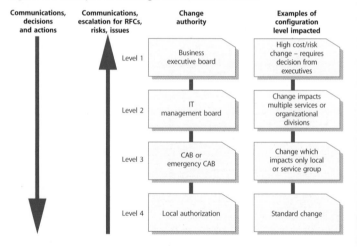

3.5.5 Configuration model

Configuration Management delivers logical and physical models of the services, assets and the infrastructure by recording the relationships between Configuration Items (CIs), as shown in Figure 3.7. This provides different views of the service and infrastructure configurations that enable different stakeholders and other processes to access information, e.g. to assess the impact of Incidents, Problems and proposed changes.

Figure 3.7 Example of a logical configuration model

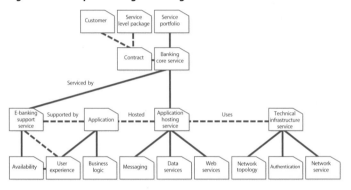

3.5.6 Service V model

Figure 3.8 provides an example of a model that can be used to represent the different configuration levels to be built and tested to deliver a service capability. The left side represents the specification of the service requirements down to the detailed Service Design. The right side focuses on the validation and test activities that are performed against the specifications defined on the left side. At each stage on the left side, there is direct involvement by the equivalent party on the right side. It shows that service validation and acceptance test planning should start with the definition of the service requirements. For example, customers who sign off the agreed service requirements will also sign off the SAC and test plan.

Figure 3.8 Service V model to represent configuration levels and testing

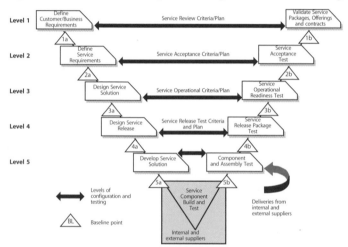

3.5.7 Release and deployment model

A service may be deployed into the production environment in a number of ways. Service Design will select the most suitable release and deployment models that include the approach, mechanisms, processes, procedures and resources required to build and deploy the release on time and within budget. Release and deployment models define:

■ Release structure – the overall structure for building a release package and the target environments

- The exit and entry criteria, including mandatory and optional deliverables and documentation for each stage
- Controlled environments required to build and test the release for each release level; there will be multiple logical and physical environments mapped to different physical environments available to the transition team
- The roles and responsibilities for each CI at each release level
- The release promotion and configuration baseline model
- Template release and deployment schedules
- Supporting systems, tools and procedures for documenting and tracking all release and deployment activities
- The handover activities and responsibilities for executing the handover and acceptance for each stage of release and deployment.

Considerations in designing the release and deployment model include activities to:

- Verify that a release complies with the SDP, architecture and related standards
- Ensure the integrity of hardware and software is protected during installation, handling, packaging and delivery
- Ensure that standard release and deployment procedures and tools are used
- Automate the delivery, distribution, installation, build and configuration audit procedures where appropriate to reduce costly manual steps
- Manage and deploy/re-deploy/remove/retire software licences
- Package and build the release package so that it can be backed out or fixed if required
- Use Configuration Management procedures, the Configuration Management System (CMS) and the Definitive Media Library (DML) to manage and control components during the build and deployment activities, e.g. to verify the prerequisites, co-requisites and post-installation requests
- Document the release and deployment steps

■ Document the deployment group or target environment that will receive the release
■ Issue service notifications.

3.5.8 Test models

Re-usable test models are developed that can be executed consistently in a repeatable way. A test model includes a test plan, what is to be tested and the test scripts that define how each element will be tested. A test model ensures that testing is executed consistently. The test scripts define the release test conditions, associated expected results and test cycles. To ensure that the process is repeatable, test models need to be well structured in a way that:

■ Provides traceability back to the requirement or design criteria
■ Enables auditing through test execution, evaluation and reporting
■ Ensures the test elements can be maintained and changed.

Examples of test models used to test a service are:

■ Service contract test model
■ Service requirements test model
■ Service level test model
■ Service test model
■ Operations test model
■ Deployment release test model
■ Deployment installation test model
■ Deployment verification test model.

Details of these models can be found in the *Service Transition* core publication.

3.5.9 The business environment

The business involvement in Service Transition is central to delivering a change successfully and maximizing value to the business. The following should be done to ensure this:

■ Align Service Transition plans and new or changed service with the customer and business organization's requirements

■ Set/re-set customer and user expectations during transition on how the performance and use of the new or changed service can enable business change and add value

■ Provide information and establish processes to enable business change projects and customers to integrate a release into their business processes and services

■ Ensure that the service can be used in accordance with the requirements and constraints specified within the service requirements in order to improve customer and stakeholder satisfaction

■ Communicate and transfer knowledge to the customers, users and stakeholders in order to increase their capability to maximize use of the new or changed service

■ Monitor and measure the use of the services and underlying applications and technology solutions during deployment and ELS in order to ensure that the service is well established before transition closure

■ Compare the actual performance of services after a transition against the predicted performance defined in Service Design, with the aim of reducing variations in service capability and performance.

From the business's perspective, this is important in order to:

■ Have a defined and agreed means for measuring the acceptability of the service, including interfaces with the service provider

■ Understand and make available the appropriate level and capability of resource to undertake service acceptance.

3.5.10 The service environment

Steps must be taken to ensure that IT staff requirements have been delivered before deployment of the service. Operations staff will use the service acceptance step to ensure that:

- Technological facilities are in place to deliver the new or changed service
- There are competent staff with appropriate skills, knowledge and resources to support the service
- Business and IT continuity has been considered
- Access is available to documentation and the Service Knowledge Management System (SKMS)
- Supporting processes and resources are in place, e.g. service desk, second-/third-line support, including third-party contracts, capacity and availability monitoring and alerting
- The operational delivery of the service meets the agreed business requirements, service standards and the required utility and warranty specifications
- The delivered operational service does not impact the delivery or service capability of any other service, unless explicitly agreed as part of the original requirements.

The Continual Service Improvement team will inherit the new or changed service into the scope of their improvement programme, and should ensure that they have sufficient understanding of its objectives, delivery components and characteristics.

3.6   SERVICE TRANSITION PROCESSES

3.6.1   Service Transition Planning and Support

Purpose

The purpose of the Transition Planning and Support activities is to:

- Plan appropriate capacity and resources to package a release, build, release, test, deploy and establish the new or changed service into production
- Provide support for the Service Transition teams and people

- Plan the changes required in a manner that ensures the integrity of all identified customer assets, service assets and configurations can be maintained as they evolve through Service Transition
- Ensure that Service Transition issues, risks and deviations are reported to the appropriate stakeholders and decision makers
- Coordinate activities across projects, suppliers and service teams where required.

Goals

The goals of Transition Planning and Support activities are to:

- Plan and coordinate the resources to ensure that the requirements of Service Strategy encoded in Service Design are effectively realized in Service Operation
- Identify, manage and control the risks of failure and disruption across transition activities.

Scope

The scope of the Service Transition Planning and Support activities includes:

- Incorporating design and operation requirements into the transition plans
- Managing and operating transition planning and support activities, the transition processes, supporting systems and tools
- Maintaining and integrating Service Transition plans across the customer, service and contract portfolios
- Managing Service Transition progress, changes, issues, risks and deviations
- Quality review of all Service Transition, release and deployment plans
- Communications with customers, users and stakeholders
- Monitoring and improving Service Transition performance.

The organization should decide the most appropriate approach to Service Transition based on the size and nature of the core and supporting services, the number and frequency of releases required, and any special needs of the users, e.g. if a phased roll-out is usually required over an extended period of time.

Strategy

The Service Transition strategy defines the overall approach to organizing Service Transition and allocating resources. The aspects to consider are:

- Purpose, goals and objectives of Service Transition
- Context, e.g. service customer, Contract Portfolios
- Scope – inclusions and exclusions
- Applicable standards, agreements, legal, regulatory and contractual requirements:
  - Internal and externals standards
  - Interpretation of legislation, industry guidelines and other externally imposed requirements
  - Agreements and contracts that apply to Service Transition
- Organizations and stakeholders involved in transition:
  - Third parties, strategic partners, suppliers and service providers
  - Customers and users
  - Service Management
  - Service provider
  - Transition organization
- Framework for Service Transition:
  - Policies, processes and practices applicable to Service Transition, including process service provider interfaces (SPIs)
  - Roles and responsibilities
  - Transition resource planning and estimation
  - Transition preparation and training requirements
  - The release and change authorization
  - Re-using the organization's experience, expertise, tools, knowledge and relevant historical data
  - Shared resources and service to support Service Transition
- Criteria:
  - Entry and exit criteria for each release stage
  - Criteria for stopping or re-starting transition activities
  - Success and failure criteria

- Identification of requirements and content of the new or changed service:
  - Services to be transitioned with target locations, customers and organizational units
  - Release definitions
  - Applicable SDP, including architectural design
  - Requirements for environments to be used, locations, organizational and technical
  - Planning and management of environments, e.g. commissioning and decommissioning
- People:
  - Assigning roles and responsibilities, including approvals
  - Assigning and scheduling training and knowledge transfer
- Approach:
  - Transition model, including Service Transition lifecycle stages
  - Plans for managing changes, assets, configurations and knowledge
  - Baseline and evaluation points
  - Configuration audit and verification points
  - Points where Requests for Change (RFCs) should be raised
  - Use of change windows
  - Transition estimation, resource and cost planning
  - Preparation for Service Transition
  - Evaluation
  - Release packaging, build, deployment and ELS
  - Error handling, correction and control
  - Management and control – recording, progress monitoring and reporting
  - Service performance and measurement system
  - Key performance indicators (KPIs) and improvement targets
- Deliverables from transition activities, including mandatory and optional documentation for each stage:
  - Transition plans
  - Change and Configuration Management Plan

- Release policy, plans and documentation
- Test plans and reports
- Build plans and documentation
- Evaluation plan and report
- Deployment plans and reports
- Transition closure report
- Schedule of milestones
- Financial requirements – budgets and funding.

The inputs are:

- Authorized RFC
- SDP
- Release package definition and design specification
- SAC.

The outputs are:

- Transition strategy
- Integrated set of Service Transition plans.

Primary KPIs for transition planning and support include:

- The number of releases implemented that met the customer's agreed requirements in terms of scope, quality, cost and release schedule (expressed as a percentage of all releases)
- Reduced variation of actual vs. predicted scope, quality, cost and time
- Increased customer and user satisfaction with plans and communications that enable the business to align their activities with the Service Transition plans
- Reduction in number of issues, risks and delays caused by inadequate planning.

3.6.2 Change Management

Changes arise for a variety of reasons:

■ Proactively, e.g. seeking business benefits such as reducing costs or improving services or increasing the ease and effectiveness of support
■ Reactively as a means of resolving Errors and adapting to changing circumstances.

Purpose

Changes should be managed to:

■ Optimize risk exposure (supporting the risk profile required by the business)
■ Minimize the severity of any impact and disruption
■ Be successful at the first attempt.

Goals

Such an approach will deliver direct benefit to the bottom line for the business by delivering early realization of benefits (or removal of risk), with a saving of money and time.

To make an appropriate response to all RFCs entails a considered approach to assessment of risk and business continuity, change impact, resource requirements, change authorization and especially to the realizable business benefit. This considered approach is essential to maintain the required balance between the need for change and the impact of the change.

Scope

The scope covers changes to the Service Portfolio as well as a baseline of service assets and CIs across the whole service lifecycle (see Figure 3.9).

Changes should be submitted as an RFC, often with an associated change proposal that provides the detail of how the change will happen, e.g. approach to implementing a legislative change. The change proposal will be based on a change model and will provide more detail about the specific change proposed.

Figure 3.9 Scope of Change and Release Management for services

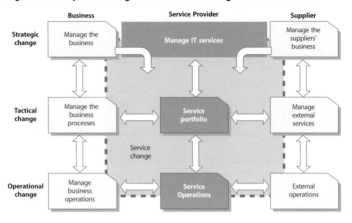

The inputs include:

- Policy and strategies for change and release
- Change proposal
- Plans – change, transition, release, deployment, test, evaluation and remediation
- Current Change Schedule (CS) and Projected Service Outage (PSO)
- Current assets or CIs, e.g. baseline, service package, release package
- As-planned configuration baseline
- Test results, test report and evaluation report.

Outputs from the process are:

- Rejected RFCs and approved RFCs
- Updates to the Service Portfolio and Service Catalogue
- Change to the services, service or infrastructure resulting from approved RFCs

- New, changed or disposed-of assets or CIs, e.g. updated configuration baseline, transferred service, service package, release package
- Revised CS and PSO
- Authorized change plans
- Change decisions and actions
- Change documents and records
- Change Management reports.

The KPIs for Change Management include:

- The number of changes implemented to services that met the customer's agreed requirements
- The benefits of change expressed as 'value of improvements made' + 'negative impacts prevented or terminated' compared with the costs of the change process
- Reduction in the number of disruptions to services, defects and re-work caused by inaccurate specification or poor or incomplete impact assessment
- Reduction in the number of unauthorized changes
- Reduction in the backlog of change requests
- Reduction in the number and percentage of unplanned changes, late changes and emergency fixes
- Change success rate (percentage of changes deemed successful at review/number of RFCs approved)
- Reduction in the number of changes where remediation (e.g. back-out) is invoked
- Reduction in the number of failed changes
- Average time to implement by urgency/priority/change type
- Incidents attributable to changes
- Variation against change estimates.

3.6.3 Service Asset and Configuration Management

Purpose

The purpose of Service Asset and Configuration Management (SACM) is to:

- Identify, control, record, report, audit and verify service assets and CIs, including versions, baselines, constituent components, their attributes, and relationships
- Account for, manage and protect the integrity of service assets and CIs (and, where appropriate, those of its customers) through the service lifecycle by ensuring that only authorized components are used and only authorized changes are made
- Protect the integrity of service assets and CIs (and, where appropriate, those of its customers) through the service lifecycle
- Ensure the integrity of the assets and configurations required to control the services and IT infrastructure by establishing and maintaining an accurate and complete CMS.

Goals

The goals of SACM are to:

- Support the business and customer's control objectives and requirements
- Support efficient and effective ITIL Service Management processes by providing accurate configuration information to enable people to make decisions at the right time, e.g. to authorize change and releases, resolve Incidents and Problems faster
- Minimize the number of quality and compliance issues caused by improper configuration of services and assets
- Optimize the service assets, IT configurations, capabilities and resources.

The objectives are to define and control the components of services and infrastructure and to maintain accurate configuration information on the historical, planned and current state of the services and infrastructure.

Scope

SACM also covers service assets across the whole service lifecycle. It provides a complete inventory of assets and who is responsible for their control, including:

■ Full lifecycle management of IT and service assets, from the point of acquisition through to disposal
■ Maintenance of the asset inventory.

Configuration Management ensures that selected components of a complete service, system or product (the configuration) are identified, have a baseline and are maintained and that changes to them are controlled. It ensures that releases into controlled environments and operational use are done on the basis of formal approvals. It also provides configuration models of the services, assets and infrastructure by recording the relationships between service assets and CIs.

The scope covers interfaces to internal and external service providers where there are assets and CIs that need to be controlled, e.g. shared assets.

SACM uses a supporting system known as the CMS, such as the example shown in Figure 3.10. The CMS holds the information for service assets and CIs within the designated scope. Some of these items will have related specifications or files that contain the contents of the item, e.g. software, document or photograph. For example, a Service CI will include the details such as supplier, cost, purchase date and renewal date for licences and maintenance contracts and the related documentation such as Service Level Agreements (SLAs) and underpinning contracts.

Figure 3.10 Example of a Configuration Management System

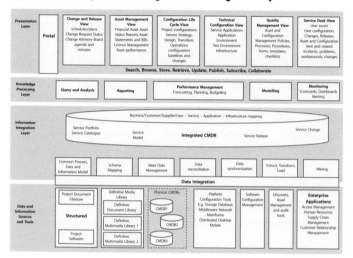

SACM supports and interfaces with every other process and activity to some degree. Examples of these include:

- Change Management – identifying the impact of proposed changes
- Financial Management – capturing key financial information such as cost, depreciation methods, owner and user (for budgeting and cost allocation), maintenance and repair costs
- IT Service Continuity Management (ITSCM) – awareness of assets that the business services depend on, control of key spares and software
- Incident/Problem/Error – providing and maintaining key diagnostic information; maintenance and provision of data to the service desk
- Availability Management's ability to detect points of failure.

Updates to asset and configuration information are triggered by RFCs, purchase orders, acquisitions and service requests.

Strategy

SACM facilitates the exchange of information with other processes and as such has few customer-facing measures. It is measured for its contribution to phases of the service lifecycle and the KPIs that affect the customer directly. In order to optimize the cost and performance of the service assets and configurations, the following measures are applicable:

- Percentage improvement in maintenance scheduling over the life of an asset (not too much, not too late)
- Assets identified as the cause of service failures
- Improved speed for Incident Management to identify faulty CIs and restore service
- Impact of Incidents and Errors affecting particular CI types, e.g. from particular suppliers or development groups, for use in improving the IT services
- Percentage re-use and redistribution of under-utilized resources and assets
- Degree of alignment of insurance premiums with business needs
- Ratio of used licences against paid-for licences (should be close to 100%)
- Average cost per user for licences (i.e. more effective charging options achieved)
- Achieved accuracy in budgets and charges for the assets utilized by each customer or business unit
- Percentage reduction in business impact of outages and Incidents caused by poor Asset and Configuration Management
- Improved audit compliance.

3.6.4 Release and Deployment Management

Purpose

The purpose of Release and Deployment Management is to:

- Define and agree release and deployment plans with customers and stakeholders

- Ensure that each release package consists of a set of related assets and service components that are compatible with each other
- Ensure that integrity of a release package and its constituent components is maintained throughout the transition activities and recorded accurately in the CMS
- Ensure that all release and deployment packages can be tracked, installed, tested, verified, and/or uninstalled or backed out if appropriate
- Ensure that organization and stakeholder change is managed during the release and deployment activities
- Record and manage deviations, risks, issues related to the new or changed service and take necessary corrective action
- Ensure that there is knowledge transfer to enable the customers and users to optimize their use of the service to support their business activities
- Ensure that skills and knowledge are transferred to operations and support staff to enable them to effectively and efficiently deliver, support and maintain the service according to required warranties and service levels.

Goals

The goal of Release and Deployment Management is to deploy releases into production and establish effective use of the service in order to deliver value to the customer and be able to hand over to Service Operation.

The objective of Release and Deployment Management is to ensure that:

- There are clear and comprehensive release and deployment plans that enable the customer and business change projects to align their activities with these plans
- A release package can be built, installed, tested and deployed efficiently to a deployment group or target environment successfully and on schedule
- A new or changed service and its enabling systems, technology and organization are capable of delivering the agreed service requirements, i.e. utilities, warranties and service levels

- There is minimal unpredicted impact on the production services, operations and support organization
- Customers, users and Service Management staff are satisfied with the Service Transition practices and outputs, e.g. user documentation and training.

Scope

The scope of Release and Deployment Management includes the processes, systems and functions to package, build, test and deploy a release into production and establish the service specified in the SDP before final handover to service operations. This scope of the release and deployment process is illustrated in Figure 3.11.

Figure 3.11 Scope of Release and Deployment

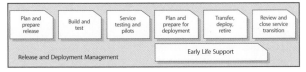

Service Transition monitors the performance of the new or changed service in ELS until the exit criteria are achieved. These include when:

- Users can use the service effectively and efficiently for their business activities
- Service owners and process owners are committed to manage and operate the service in accordance with the service model, performance standards and processes
- Service delivery is managed and controlled across any service provider interfaces
- Service levels and service performance standards are being consistently achieved without unexpected variation before formal handover to Service Operation
- SLAs are finalized and signed off by senior management and customers

- Unexpected variations in the performance of the service and customer assets, such as changes in residual risks, are monitored, reported and managed appropriately
- Checking that training and knowledge transfer activities are completed by obtaining positive confirmation from the target audience. This may be in the form of competency tests
- The service release, the SLA, other agreements and any contractual deliverables are signed off.

Strategy

The release process commences with receipt of an approved RFC to deploy a production-ready release package. Deployment commences with receipt of an approved RFC to deploy a release package to a target deployment group or environment, e.g. business unit, customer group and/or service unit.

The inputs are:

- Authorized RFC
- Service Level Package (SLP)
- SDP, including service model and SAC
- IT service continuity plan and related business continuity plan
- Service Management and operations plans and standards
- Technology and procurement standards and catalogues
- Acquired service assets and components and their documentation
- Build models and plans
- Environment requirements and specifications for build, test, release, training, disaster recovery, pilot and deployment
- Release policy and release design from Service Design
- Release and deployment models including template plans
- Exit and entry criteria for each stage of release and deployment.

The outputs are:

- Release and deployment plan
- Completed RFCs for the release and deployment activities
- Service notification
- Updated Service Catalogue with the relevant information about the new or changed service
- New tested service capability and environment
- New or changed service and ITIL Service Management documentation
- Updated service package that defines the requirements from the business/customer for the service
- Updated SLP that defines the Service Level Requirements (SLRs), e.g. hours of service, business critical services and periods, service targets
- SLA, underpinning Operational Level Agreements (OLAs) and contracts
- Service model that describes the structure and dynamics of how the service is operated and managed
- New or changed service reports
- Tested continuity plans
- Validated service capacity plan
- Complete and accurate CI list with an audit trail for the CIs in the release package and also the new or changed service and infrastructure configurations
- Deployment-ready release package (with a baseline) – for future deployments
- Service Transition report.

The KPIs are:

- Variance from service performance required by customers (minimal and reducing)
- Number of Incidents against the service (low and reducing)
- Increased customer and user satisfaction with the services delivered
- Decreased customer dissatisfaction – service issues resulting from poorly tested or untested services increases negative perception

- Reduced resources and costs to diagnose and fix Incidents and Problems in deployment and production
- Increased adoption of the Service Transition common framework of standards, reusable processes and supporting documentation
- Reduced discrepancies in configuration audits compared with the real world.

3.6.5 Service Validation and Testing

Purpose

Testing is applied throughout the service lifecycle and quality assures every aspect of a service and the service providers' capability, resources and capacity to deliver a service and/or service release successfully.

Figure 3.12 Scope of Testing Activities

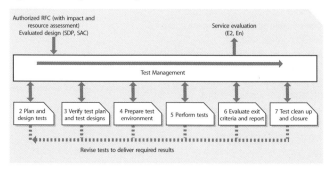

Goals

Testing directly supports the release and deployment process by ensuring that appropriate levels of testing are performed during the release, build and deployment activities. An example of testing activities is shown in Figure 3.12.

Scope

Effective validation and testing focuses on whether the service will deliver as required. This is based on the perspective of those who will use, deliver, deploy, manage and operate the service.

The key inputs to the process are:

■ Service package and SLPs
■ Service provider interface definitions
■ SDP

The direct output from testing is the report delivered to the service evaluation team setting out:

■ Configuration baseline of the testing environment
■ Testing carried out (including options chosen and constraints encountered)
■ Results from those tests and analysis of the results.

Other outputs include:

■ Updated data, information and knowledge to be added to the SKMS
■ Test Incidents, Problems and Error records.

The effectiveness of testing in delivering to the business can be judged through the following KPIs:

■ Early validation that the service will deliver the predicted value that enables early correction
■ Reduction in the impact of Incidents and Errors in live running that are attributable to newly transitioned services
■ More effective use of resource and involvement from the customer/business
■ Reduced delays in testing that impact the business
■ Increased mutual understanding of the new/changed service
■ Clear understanding of roles and responsibilities associated with the new or changed service between the stakeholders

■ Cost and resources required from user and customer involvement (e.g. user acceptance testing).
■ Economy of the testing process, including:
  – Test planning, preparation, execution
  – Cost of unplanned and unbudgeted overtime
  – Cost of fixing Errors in live operation compared to fixing Errors early in the lifecycle
  – Operational cost improvements associated with reducing Errors in new or changed services.

3.6.6 Evaluation

Purpose

The evaluation of new or changed services defined by Service Design, during deployment and before final transition to Service Operation, includes:

■ Evaluating the actual performance of any service change against its anticipated performance
■ Ensuring that expectations are realistic
■ Identifying any reasons why production performance does not meet what was expected, including the risk profile.

Scope

The inputs into evaluation are:

■ Service package, SDP and SAC
■ Test plan, results and report.

The output is an Evaluation report for Change Management.

The customer/business KPIs are:

■ Variance from service performance required by customers (minimal and reducing)
■ Number of Incidents against the service (low and reducing).

The internal KPIs include:

■ Number of failed designs that have been transitioned (zero)
■ Cycle time to perform an evaluation (low and reducing).

3.6.7 Knowledge Management

Scope

The scope of Knowledge Management includes oversight of the management of knowledge, the information and data from which that knowledge derives, across the lifecycle. Knowledge Management is typically displayed within the data–information–knowledge–wisdom (DIKW) structure, as illustrated in Figure 3.13.

Figure 3.13 The flow from data to wisdom

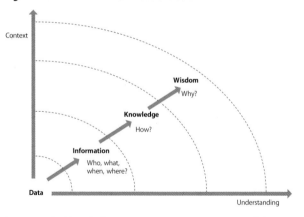

Inputs to the Knowledge Management process consist of the captured data and information from across the lifecycle, e.g.:

■ Errors detected during transition
■ Adaptability and accessibility of the service design.

Generated wisdom, and the decisions taken based upon that wisdom, constitute the outputs from the process.

Typical KPIs for an IT service provider's contribution are:

- Successful implementation and early-life operation of new and changed services with few knowledge-related errors
- Increased responsiveness to changing business demands, e.g. higher percentage of queries solved via the SKMS
- Improved accessibility and management of standards and policies
- Knowledge dissemination
- Reduced time and effort required to support and maintain services
- Reduced time to find information for diagnoses and fixing
- Reduced dependency on personnel for knowledge.

Knowledge rests on the management of the information and data that underpins it. To be effective this process requires an understanding of some key process inputs such as:

- How the data and information will be used
- The knowledge necessary for the decisions that must be made
- The conditions that need to be monitored (changing external and internal circumstances, ranging from end-user demand, legal requirements through to weather forecasts)
- What data is available (could be captured), as well as rejecting possible data capture as infeasible; this input may trigger justification for expenditure or changes in working practices designed to facilitate the capture of relevant data that would otherwise not be available
- The cost of capturing and maintaining data, and the value that data is likely to bring, bearing in mind the negative impact of data overload on effective knowledge transfer
- Applicable policies, legislation, standards and other requirements
- Intellectual property rights and copyright issues.

The key to Knowledge Management is understanding how the SKMS integrates with the architecture and other systems utilized throughout the lifecycle (see Figure 3.14).

Figure 3.14 Relationship of the CMDB, the CMS and the SKMS

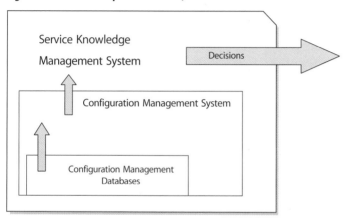

3.7 PRACTICAL TRANSITIONS

In today's ever-changing world, Service Transition will inevitably be dealing with the transfer of service(s) from in-house to outsource provider, from outsource provider back to in-house, or from one outsource provider to another. It is essential that, whichever direction the responsibility for service provision is going, the transition is well managed and that the new or changed services are delivered to requirements.

Transferring the control of services includes the following circumstances:

- Out to a new supplier, e.g. outsourcing, off-shoring
- From one supplier to another
- Back in from a supplier, e.g. insourcing
- To or from an external service provider
- Moving to a shared service provision, e.g. partial outsource of some processes
- Multiple suppliers, e.g. smart-sourcing
- Joint venture/secondment
- Partnering
- Down-sizing, up-sizing (right-sizing)
- Merger and acquisition.

3.7.1 In-house to outsource provider

Transitioning services from in-house provision to an outsource provider is an emotional rollercoaster for all involved, as it usually results in job losses or changes in responsibilities. It is therefore even more critical that Service Transition communication is considered paramount, and that the roles and responsibilities of all involved are clearly understood.

Key considerations are:

- Direct involvement of impacted staff wherever possible
- Clear communication from Service Strategy of the business drivers
- Clear understanding from Service Design of the selection criteria and the rationale for the selected supplier
- Published plans that do not change unless absolutely unavoidable
- Clear direction for the current service resources, including human resources, e.g. retirement of service assets and CIs
- Clear understanding by the business of the potential impact of change
- Supplier capability to meet the ongoing customer demands
- Service utility and warranty requirements
- Responsiveness to change requirements

- Delivery requirements
- ELS.

3.7.2 Outsource provider to in-house

Insourcing service provision is more common now, due to the high number of mergers and acquisitions. What were previously considered as non-core services suddenly appear to be core, or are realigned to fit the new business model. Transitioning services from an external supplier is generally regarded as an opportunity, unless of course the service is considered to be troublesome on outdated infrastructure and architecture.

Key considerations are:

- Resource requirements – transition, early-life and operations support
- Knowledge Management
- SACM, including audit and validation
- Service transition capabilities – timescales and operational readiness both by incumbent and internally.

3.7.3 Transition of outsource supplier

Transition of service provision from one outsource provider to another is very common as businesses take advantage of the competitive markets. It is often that the perceived pain of transition is outweighed by the financial gains of the new contract. Most outsourcers accept the transition to an alternative supplier and act in professional manner throughout in the hope that they will one day regain the service contract.

Key considerations are:

- Maintaining transition control between the providers
- Communication between all parties
- Audit and validation of SACM pre- and post transition
- Risks and issues management
- Knowledge Management

- Incoming supplier capability
- Service Transition capabilities; timescales and operational readiness by both incumbent and new supplier
- ELS.

3.8 CHALLENGES, OPPORTUNITIES AND OPTIMIZATION

The complexity of services across the supply chain is increasing, and this leads to challenges for any service provider that implements new services or changes existing services. IT within e-business not only supports the primary business processes, but is part of the primary business processes.

This prime position brings a wide range of challenges to successful Service Transition, such as:

- Managing many contacts, interfaces and relationships through Service Transition, including a variety of different customers, users, programmes, projects, suppliers and partners
- Harmonization and integration of the processes and disciplines that impact Service Transition, e.g. finance, engineering, human resource management
- Differences among the legacy systems, new technology and human elements that result in unknown dependencies and are risky to change
- Achieving a balance between maintaining a stable production environment and being responsive to the business needs for changing the services
- Creating an environment that fosters standardization, simplification and knowledge sharing
- Being an enabler of business change and, therefore, an integral component of the business change programmes
- Establishing 'who is doing what, when and where' and 'who should be doing what, when and where'
- Developing a culture that encourages people to collaborate and work effectively together, and an atmosphere that fosters the cultural shifts necessary to get buy-in from people

- Developing standard performance measures and measurement methods across projects and suppliers
- Ensuring that the quality of delivery and support matches the business use of new technology
- Ensuring that the Service Transition time and budget is not impacted by events earlier in the service lifecycle (e.g. budget cuts)
- Understanding, and being able to assess, the balance between managing risk and taking risks as it affects the overall strategy of the organization and potential mismatch between project risks and business risk.

Implementing effective Service Transition policies, process, procedures and systems will create the following opportunities for the customer, the business and IT by:

- Proactively improving quality of new and existing services
- Getting closer to project delivery from the outset, thereby improving communication, understanding of delivery and better enabling IT to meet requirements
- Adding value to the business by identifying opportunities for business improvement
- Responding to market opportunities in a structured and proven manner
- Creating more business opportunities by demonstrating better control of assets and services.

3.9 KEY MESSAGES AND LESSONS

Key messages and guidance when looking to implement Service Transition are as follows:

- The scale of change is not important; what is important is understanding that all change should follow the ITIL Service Lifecycle to ensure delivery of the best possible benefit to the business

- Use previous experience to ensure that Service Transition practices and processes are constantly reviewed and improved; encode this experience in re-useable, understandable Service Transition models and documentation that can be shared and re-used
- An organization with a mixture of centralized, distributed and localized infrastructure should consider piloting each type separately, as the extra cost and complications are worth it.

When designing Service Transition, consider how agreed policies, standards and legislation will constrain the design:

- Communication is critical throughout any transition, both internally and externally, with customers, stakeholders and suppliers
- Although Service Transition should deliver an overall net benefit to the organization (or they should be revisited and revised), nonetheless they do require funding, and the Service Transition strategy should address the source and control of financial provision
- Service Transition needs to take a broader view across projects, combining transitions and releases to make the best use of available resources
- If implementing Service Transition into an organization means installing formal processes that were not there before, the cultural change is significant. Experience shows that staff working in Change Management, and even those evangelizing change among others, are potentially as resistant to change in their own areas as anyone else.

When delivering business change that involves many different departments, ensure that ownership for each component of the overall service package is defined, and subsequently management responsibility is clear.

4   Further guidance and contact points

Other frameworks or methodologies that have valid contributions to make to Service Transition and have synergy with ITIL are listed below.

Programme and project management

Many organizations adopt programme and project management methodologies and frameworks to manage business and technology change. Service Transition personnel may be part of a project team or may work with programmes and project teams. Further guidance on these topics includes:

- *Managing Successful Programmes*, Office of Government Commerce, 2007 (The Stationery Office, Norwich)
- *Managing Successful Projects with PRINCE2*, Office of Government Commerce, 2007 (The Stationery Office, Norwich)
- *A Guide to the Project Management Body of Knowledge* (PMBOK® Guides), 3rd edn, Project Management Institute, 2004 (Project Management Institute, Pennsylvania).

Management of Risk

Management of Risk (M_o_R®) is a framework and standard methodology for the management of risk. It provides guidance on the principles, the approach and the processes that should be used in the management of risk within an organization. The guidance supports the management of risk that is essential during Service Transition.

Service oriented architecture

The service oriented architecture (SOA) approach is used by many organizations to improve their effectiveness and efficiency in the provision of IT services. SOA brings value and agility to an organization by encouraging the development of 'self-contained' services that are reusable, promoting a flexible approach to the development of 'shared services'. The structures within SOA can help in designing configuration models and the CMS.

Control Objectives for Information and related Technology

The Control Objectives for Information and related Technology (COBIT) framework, from the IT Governance Institute (ITGI), provides a framework of guidance for IT audit and security personnel.

The current version of COBIT, edition 4, includes 34 High Level Control Objectives, 10 of which are grouped under the 'Plan and Organise Domain' and seven within 'Acquire and Implement Domain' many of which map quite closely onto ITIL's Service Transition lifecycle stage.

Quality management

There are distinct advantages of implementing service management within an organization as part of its quality management system. If an organization has a formal quality management system, such as ISO9000, Six Sigma, Total Quality Management (TQM), etc., then this can be used to assess progress regularly and drive forward agreed service improvement initiatives through regular reviews and reporting.

ISO/IEC 20000

Organizations can seek independent accreditation against the International Standards Organization standard ISO/IEC 20000. The standard is supported by a series of publications from the British Standards Institution (BSI) titled 'Achieving ISO/IEC 20000'.

ISO/IEC 20000 initially mapped to the prior *Service Support* and *Service Delivery* publications of ITIL. It continues to map well to ITIL Service Management Practices today and many organizations use the ITIL Service Lifecycle to help them to achieve the standard. Related international standards are:

■ ISO/IEC 19770 Software Asset Management – Processes
■ ISO/IEC 27001 Information Security Management Systems – Requirements.

Capability Maturity Model Integration

The Capability Maturity Model® Integration (CMMI) is a process improvement approach developed by the Software Engineering Institute (SEI) of Carnegie Mellon University in Philadelphia. CMMI helps integrate traditionally separate organizational functions, set process improvement goals and priorities, provide guidance for quality processes and provide a point of reference for appraising current processes.

Balanced Scorecard

The Balanced Scorecard provides a clear prescription as to what companies should measure in order to 'balance' various perspectives:

- Learning and Growth
- Business Process
- Customer
- Financial.

It is valuable to develop metrics, collect data and analyse it. This is useful during Service Transition when evaluating actual performance against predicted performance.